Lonely planet KIDS

CW01391280

Explorer's NATURE JOURNAL

A Guide to Discovery, Creativity and Outdoor Adventure!

Written by Emma Carlson Berne

Illustrated by Kelly Abeln

CONTENTS

HELLO, NATURE!

Squirrels burying acorns, ants moving their eggs, plants pushing up through the dirt — nature is a busy place. You'll always find something to see, smell or touch. Is it autumn? Are the leaves dry and crispy? Or is it winter, when you might smell ice and snow in the air? How about summer or spring, when bees buzz around the flowers?

Taking a journal with you outside is like taking a friend. You can write about and draw what you see and hear and touch. You can draw maps of your routes or the routes of the creatures around you — either right then and there, or later, using your notes. These notes and drawings can help you see nature more *mindfully* — to really notice the natural world around you.

You can go outside with this journal in all seasons — even wet and cold ones — and at different times of the day. You can even try going out at night, with your torch and a trusted grown-up. Keep you eyes peeled and you might ee birds flying in the blue sky, squirrels digging in the dirt and flowers pushing up from the grass. The world of nature is calling you — so get out there!

SPRING

SUMMER

AUTUMN

WINTER

HOW TO WORK THIS BOOK

This journal is your guide through nature, with lots of places for you to record what you notice and what you think. As you leaf through the pages that follow, you'll find blank spaces for drawing, writing and mapping. When you see prompts that ask where you saw something, you can write in things like, I saw a bird in a tree or on the ground, for example. In some places you'll be asked to circle one or more items from a selection instead.

FILL IN

The weather right now is: _____

_____ Sunny, warm, humid _____

CIRCLE ONE

It is smaller than an apple: (yes)   no

Here's where I am right now:

(back garden)   front garden   porch   deck

CHECK ALL THAT APPLY

The animal has:

☐ WINGS   ☐ FEATHERS   ☒ A TAIL   ☒ PAWS

☒ FUR   ☐ SCALES   ☒ CLAWS

You'll also see an activity page at the end of each section. This is your chance to get creative with crafts, games and other projects.

PLANT MEMORY

Play Plant Memory! Make your own memory game using various plant parts: leaves, seeds, berries or small fruits, and flowers.

YOU WILL NEED

- A pair of leaves, a pair of seeds, a pair of berries or small fruits, and a pair of flowers
- 8 identical small boxes or containers with lids, or 8 halves of plastic eggs
- A partner

TIP
Before collecting any objects, check with an adult to make sure it's okay to do so.

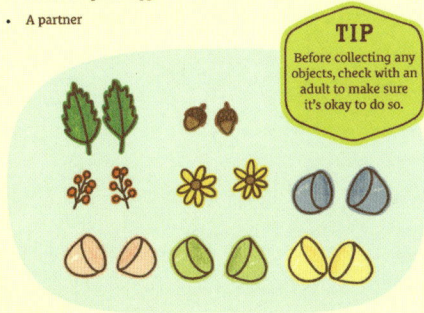

HOW TO PLAY

- Put one object in each box or under each egg half.
- Mix up the boxes or egg halves.
- Take turns peeking in two boxes or under two eggs at a time.
- If the objects match, the peeker keeps the objects. If not, it's the other person's turn.
- At the end of the game, each of you counts your objects. The person with the most is the winner!

MIX   MIX

MATCH!

NO MATCH!

Remember that you're going to be doing a lot of writing outside, so think carefully about your writing tools. Markers and pencils are great for outside work. Pens sometimes don't work so well in cold weather, so if it's icy outside, leave your ballpoint at home. You also might want to bring a large, flat book to rest your journal on when you're writing. Big picture books are great for this.

You can take this journal with you on hikes and nature outings, of course, but you can also just stash it in your backpack when you leave for school or a friend's house. Nature is great in tiny doses as well as larger ones. After all, you never know when you might see an exciting insect or have an encounter with a squirrel. You can whip out your journal and make note of what you see right then and there.

GEARING UP!

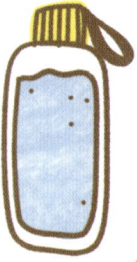

The world of nature is waiting for you — but hang on! Let's pack a kit bag first. Here are some things you'll want to take with you on each nature outing. After all, who wants to leave the house without their emergency granola bar?

Book or notebook with a stiff cover to write on, and pens, markers or pencils. You could also use a clipboard.

Rain jacket with a hood for wet days and a warm jacket, hat and gloves for cold days. For hot days, don't forget your baseball cap or sun hat.

Sunscreen. Nothing ruins a fun nature outing like sunburn.

Bug spray. Mosquito bites? No thanks.

Water bottle and a healthy snack. You might need some fuel while outdoors, but avoid sugary snacks. Otherwise, you might be sharing your food with the insects, too.

Long trousers and a long-sleeved shirt. Even when it's hot, long trousers and long sleeves are a good idea. You can keep away the sun's rays and the bugs at the same time!

Small first aid kit, with bandages, tweezers, alcohol wipes and hydrocortisone cream (it helps soothe insect bites). Take that, thorns!

Torch, just in case you and your grown-up are out past dark.

Small backpack to keep everything in!

Your eyes, ears, nose and fingers. Don't forget these! They're the most important pieces of gear you have.

STAY SAFE OUT THERE!

A nature outing can be fun, exciting, relaxing and beautiful. Let's make sure it's also safe! Always take a trusty grown-up with you. Do they have their mobile phone? Ask them, just to make sure.

Check the weather before you leave home. If there's a cold weather warning or a heat warning, plan your outing for a different day. Thunder and lightning in the forecast? Stay home and enjoy nature from your window.

Explore in a safe area, such as a back garden, park, or nature trail. Always stay on the marked path and obey the instructions on the signs. Those rules are there to keep you safe!

If you get pricked, scratched or stung, stay calm. Ask your grown-up for help and break out your first aid kit. After you treat your wound, decide if you feel okay to continue with your outing or if you need to head home.

Did you find a tick (oh, yuck!) on yourself? Don't pull it off, even though you'll want to. Ask your grown-up to carefully remove the tick with tweezers. Clean the area and save the tick in a plastic bag. Sometimes, your doctor might want to see the tick later.

PAWS OR CLAWS?
ALL ABOUT ANIMAL TRACKS

Footprints, claw prints, paw prints — checking out animal tracks can be a great way to see what's scampering around near you. Look for mud patches, wet sand or snow — then see if you can spy the tracks.

CLAWS

Songbirds, like sparrows, finches and blackbirds, have small, delicate tracks, with three toes pointing forwards. The tracks are in pairs, since these birds hop rather than walk.

Raptors, such as hawks, eagles, kites and owls, use their large claws, called talons, to grip prey. You can see the talons, long and sharp, on the ends of their toes.

Two toes at the front and two toes at the back? You're looking at woodpecker tracks.

Webbed feet mean a water bird — perhaps a gull, goose or duck.

Wading birds near water, like sandpipers, leave prints similar to a songbird's but in a straight line, since they walk rather than hop.

PAWS

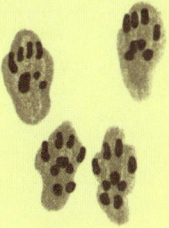

Tracks in a square or almost side by side are most likely left by a squirrel.

Rabbits leave tracks in a "Y" pattern, with small oval paw marks.

A webbed print with five toes no claw marks visible? That's an otter!

Fox tracks will have four toes facing forward. Look for a big space between the pad and the toes.

If you see long claw marks and five toe prints, with a wide pad, you've found badger prints.

Dogs and coyotes (and wolves!) share similar tracks, with pads and claw marks.

AND HOOVES!

Deer hooves are cloven, meaning they are divided into two sections like small ovals.

ANIMALS ALL AROUND US

Go outside and get your eyes and ears ready (maybe your nose, too!). Animals of all sorts share our natural world — so let's start exploring.

Animals often stay hidden from humans, so you're going to need all your investigative powers. Stand or sit quietly in your observation spot. Look up into the sky or the treetops. Look down at the ground. Now, close your eyes and listen. Do you hear birds singing? Or the scurrying of a squirrel through the leaves? Note down your observations in the pages that follow.

MY OBSERVATIONS...

Animal name: _____

_____

Where I saw it: _____

_____

This is what the animal was doing: _____

_____

_____

The weather that day was: _____

_____

The animal has:

☐ WINGS   ☐ FEATHERS   ☐ A TAIL   ☐ PAWS

☐ FUR   ☐ SCALES   ☐ CLAWS

The animal's colour is: _____

_____

It is bigger than an apple: yes   no

It is smaller than an apple: yes   no

It is *a lot* smaller than a grape: yes   no

Here is a picture of the animal:

MY OBSERVATIONS...

Animal name: _____

_____

Where I saw it: _____

_____

This is what the animal was doing: _____

_____

_____

The weather that day was: _____

_____

The animal has:

☐ WINGS ☐ FEATHERS ☐ A TAIL ☐ PAWS

☐ FUR ☐ SCALES ☐ CLAWS

The animal's colour is: _____

_____

It is bigger than an apple: yes   no

It is smaller than an apple: yes   no

It is *a lot* smaller than a grape: yes   no

Here is a picture of the animal:

MY OBSERVATIONS...

Animal name: _____

_____

Where I saw it: _____

_____

This is what the animal was doing: _____

_____

_____

The weather that day was: _____

_____

The animal has:

☐ WINGS   ☐ FEATHERS   ☐ A TAIL   ☐ PAWS

☐ FUR   ☐ SCALES   ☐ CLAWS

The animal's colour is: _____

_____

It is bigger than an apple: yes   no

It is smaller than an apple: yes   no

It is _a lot_ smaller than a grape: yes   no

Here is a picture of the animal:

MY OBSERVATIONS...

Animal name: _____

_____

Where I saw it: _____

_____

This is what the animal was doing: _____

_____

_____

The weather that day was: _____

_____

The animal has:

☐ WINGS   ☐ FEATHERS   ☐ A TAIL   ☐ PAWS

☐ FUR   ☐ SCALES   ☐ CLAWS

The animal's colour is: _____

_____

It is bigger than an apple: yes   no

It is smaller than an apple: yes   no

It is *a lot* smaller than a grape: yes   no

Here is a picture of the animal:

MY OBSERVATIONS...

Animal name: _____

_____

Where I saw it: _____

_____

This is what the animal was doing: _____

_____

_____

The weather that day was: _____

_____

The animal has:

☐ WINGS   ☐ FEATHERS   ☐ A TAIL   ☐ PAWS

☐ FUR   ☐ SCALES   ☐ CLAWS

The animal's colour is: _____

_____

It is bigger than an apple: yes   no

It is smaller than an apple: yes   no

It is *a lot* smaller than a grape: yes   no

Here is a picture of the animal:

MY OBSERVATIONS...

Animal name: _____

_____

Where I saw it: _____

_____

This is what the animal was doing: _____

_____

_____

The weather that day was: _____

_____

The animal has:

☐ WINGS	☐ FEATHERS	☐ A TAIL	☐ PAWS
☐ FUR	☐ SCALES	☐ CLAWS	

The animal's colour is: _____

_____

It is bigger than an apple: yes   no

It is smaller than an apple: yes   no

It is *a lot* smaller than a grape: yes   no

Here is a picture of the animal:

ANIMAL SCAVENGER HUNT

See if you can check off all the boxes in this back garden animal scavenger hunt.

I'm an animal observer! I noticed an animal...

☐ **WITH FUR**

☐ **WITH FEATHERS**

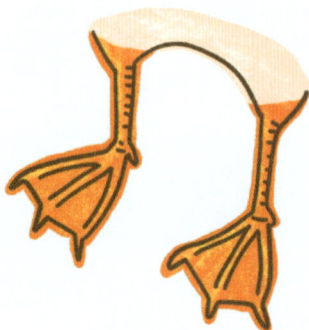

☐ **WITH TWO FEET**

☐ **WITH FOUR FEET**

☐ **FLYING, RUNNING OR JUMPING**

☐ **WITH A TAIL**

☐ **EATING**

☐ **SINGING, BARKING OR SQUEALING**

OUR GREEN GLOBE: PLANTS!

Flowery, spiky, leafy, tiny, giant — the world of plants can be overwhelming! And different plants live in different ecosystems. Hot, dry places might have cactuses and succulents. These plants don't need much water. Ferns and moss might grow in wetter places. In the forest, tall trees reach for the sunlight, and in sunny spots, grasses and shrubs grow.

Add plants to your journal using some of these easy identification tips!

BUSHES AND SHRUBS

Is your plant thick, with many branches and leaves? Is it shorter than a tree? It's a bush or a shrub.

LICHEN AND MOSS

Does your plant hug the ground or the rock, like a little rug? You're looking at lichen or moss.

VINES

Does your plant hang down or twine around a trellis or another plant? You've found a vine!

CACTUSES

Is your plant covered in clusters of sharp spines? It's a cactus.

MY OBSERVATIONS...

I saw my plant in: _____

_____

The season was: _____

My plant was growing in: *(circle one)*

sun   shade   a little bit of both

My plant has flowers: yes   no

My plant has fruit or berries: yes   no

This is a picture of my plant:

This is a picture of one leaf from my plant:

My plant smells like: _____

_____

My plant has seeds: yes   no

The seeds look like this:

MY OBSERVATIONS...

I saw my plant in: _____

_____

The season was: _____

My plant was growing in: _(circle one)_

sun   shade   a little bit of both

My plant has flowers: yes   no

My plant has fruit or berries: yes   no

This is a picture of my plant:

This is a picture of one leaf from my plant:

My plant smells like: _____

My plant has seeds: yes   no

The seeds look like this:

MY OBSERVATIONS...

I saw my plant in: _____

_____

The season was: _____

My plant was growing in: *(circle one)*

sun   shade   a little bit of both

My plant has flowers: yes   no

My plant has fruit or berries: yes   no

This is a picture of my plant:

This is a picture of one leaf from my plant:

My plant smells like: _____

_____

My plant has seeds: yes   no

The seeds look like this:

MY OBSERVATIONS...

I saw my plant in: _____

_____

The season was: _____

My plant was growing in: *(circle one)*

sun   shade   a little bit of both

My plant has flowers: yes   no

My plant has fruit or berries: yes   no

This is a picture of my plant:

This is a picture of one leaf from my plant:

My plant smells like: _____

My plant has seeds: yes   no

The seeds look like this:

MY OBSERVATIONS...

I saw my plant in: _____

_____

The season was: _____

My plant was growing in: *(circle one)*

sun   shade   a little bit of both

My plant has flowers: yes   no

My plant has fruit or berries: yes   no

This is a picture of my plant:

This is a picture of one leaf from my plant:

My plant smells like: _____

_____

My plant has seeds: yes   no

The seeds look like this:

PLANT MEMORY

Play Plant Memory! Make your own memory game using various plant parts: leaves, seeds, berries or small fruits, and flowers.

YOU WILL NEED

- A pair of leaves, a pair of seeds, a pair of berries or small fruits, and a pair of flowers

- 8 identical small boxes or containers with lids, or 8 halves of plastic eggs

- A partner

TIP
Before collecting any objects, check with an adult to make sure it's okay to do so.

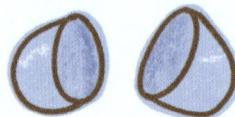

HOW TO PLAY

- Put one object in each box or under each egg half.

- Mix up the boxes or egg halves.

- Take turns peeking in two boxes or under two eggs at a time.

- If the objects match, the peeker keeps the objects. If not, it's the other person's turn.

- At the end of the game, each of you counts your objects. The person with the most is the winner!

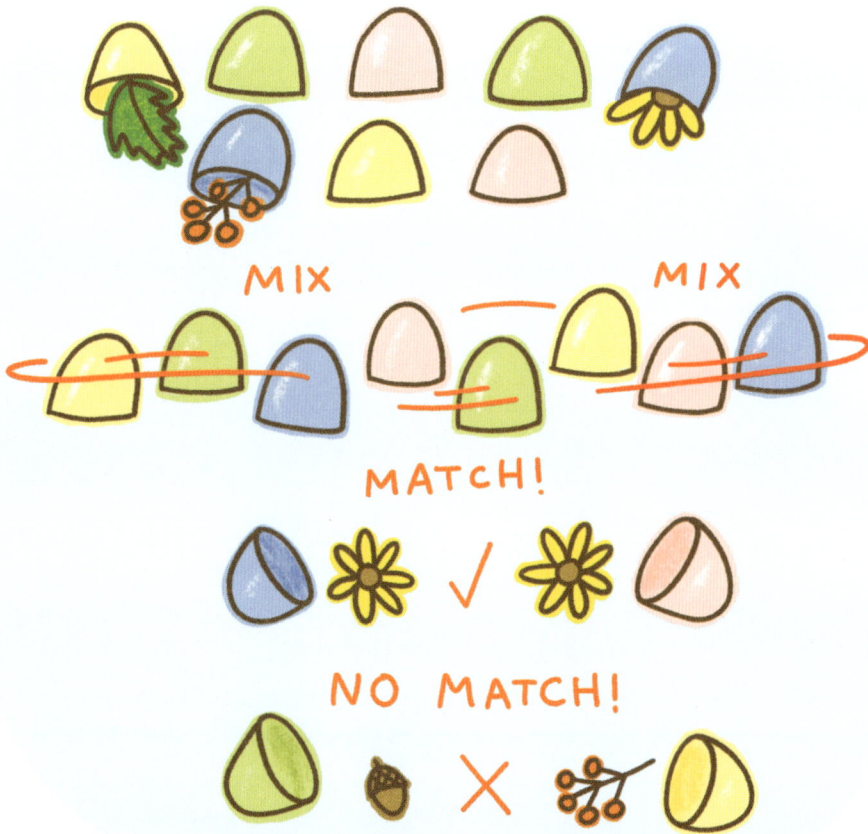

MIX   MIX

MATCH!

√

NO MATCH!

X

TALL TREES

You don't have to climb trees to get up close to them. Observing these giants from the ground can be just as fun. Ecosystems all over the world depend on trees. Their roots keep soil from blowing away. Birds, insects and other animals eat the trees' seeds and fruit and live in their branches and trunks. Trees are air cleaners, too. They take in harmful carbon dioxide and give off oxygen. Grab your journal and head outside. Let's spend some time with these nature superstars!

MY OBSERVATIONS...

I saw my tree in or by: _____

_____

When I saw my tree, the season was: _____

My tree has leaves in the winter. It's an evergreen: yes   no

My tree is bare in the winter. It's deciduous: yes   no

My tree is taller than a house: yes   no

Here is a picture of my tree:

Here is a picture of one of my tree's leaves:

MY TREE HAS . . .

Narrow, needlelike leaves   **OR**   Wide, flat leaves

CONIFER   **BROADLEAF**

 One leaf on one leaf stem   **OR**   Many leaves on one leaf stem

SIMPLE   **COMPOUND**

 Parts sticking out from the middle of the leaves   **OR**   Same edge all the way around

LOBED   **UNLOBED**

In my tree, I see:

☐ A NEST   ☐ INSECTS   ☐ BIRDS

☐ A HOLE   ☐ OTHER ANIMALS

My tree's bark is: smooth   rough

MY OBSERVATIONS...

I saw my tree in or by: _____

_____

When I saw my tree, the season was: _____

My tree has leaves in the winter. It's an evergreen: yes   no

My tree is bare in the winter. It's deciduous: yes   no

My tree is taller than a house: yes   no

Here is a picture of my tree:

Here is a picture of one of my tree's leaves:

MY TREE HAS . . .

Narrow, needlelike leaves **OR** Wide, flat leaves

↓ ↓

CONIFER **BROADLEAF**

↙ ↘

 One leaf on one leaf stem **OR** Many leaves on one leaf stem

↓ ↓

SIMPLE **COMPOUND**

↓

 Parts sticking out from the middle of the leaves **OR** Same edge all the way around

↙ ↘

LOBED **UNLOBED**

In my tree, I see:

☐ A NEST ☐ INSECTS ☐ BIRDS

☐ A HOLE ☐ OTHER ANIMALS

My tree's bark is: smooth rough

47

MY OBSERVATIONS...

I saw my tree in or by: _____

_____

When I saw my tree, the season was: _____

My tree has leaves in the winter. It's an evergreen: yes   no

My tree is bare in the winter. It's deciduous: yes   no

My tree is taller than a house: yes   no

Here is a picture of my tree:

Here is a picture of one of my tree's leaves:

MY TREE HAS . . .

Narrow,
needlelike leaves

OR

Wide, flat leaves

↓

CONIFER

↓

BROADLEAF

One leaf on
one leaf stem

OR

Many leaves on
one leaf stem

↓

SIMPLE

↓

COMPOUND

↓

Parts sticking out
from the middle
of the leaves

OR

Same edge
all the way
around

↓

LOBED

↓

UNLOBED

In my tree, I see:

☐ A NEST ☐ INSECTS ☐ BIRDS

☐ A HOLE ☐ OTHER ANIMALS

My tree's bark is: smooth rough

MY OBSERVATIONS...

I saw my tree in or by: _____

_____

When I saw my tree, the season was: _____

My tree has leaves in the winter. It's an evergreen: yes   no

My tree is bare in the winter. It's deciduous: yes   no

My tree is taller than a house: yes   no

Here is a picture of my tree:

Here is a picture of one of my tree's leaves:

MY TREE HAS . . .

Narrow,
needlelike leaves

OR

Wide, flat leaves

↓

CONIFER

↓

BROADLEAF

One leaf on
one leaf stem

OR

Many leaves on
one leaf stem

↓

SIMPLE

↓

COMPOUND

Parts sticking out
from the middle
of the leaves

OR

Same edge
all the way
around

↓

LOBED

↓

UNLOBED

In my tree, I see:

☐ A NEST ☐ INSECTS ☐ BIRDS

☐ A HOLE ☐ OTHER ANIMALS

My tree's bark is: smooth rough

MY OBSERVATIONS...

I saw my tree in or by: _____

_____

When I saw my tree, the season was: _____

My tree has leaves in the winter. It's an evergreen: yes   no

My tree is bare in the winter. It's deciduous: yes   no

My tree is taller than a house: yes   no

Here is a picture of my tree:

Here is a picture of one of my tree's leaves:

MY TREE HAS . . .

Narrow, needlelike leaves   **OR**   Wide, flat leaves

CONIFER

BROADLEAF

 One leaf on one leaf stem   **OR**   Many leaves on one leaf stem

SIMPLE   **COMPOUND**

 Parts sticking out from the middle of the leaves   **OR**   Same edge all the way around

LOBED   **UNLOBED**

In my tree, I see:

☐ A NEST   ☐ INSECTS   ☐ BIRDS

☐ A HOLE   ☐ OTHER ANIMALS

My tree's bark is: smooth   rough

MAKE A LEAF RUBBING

Make some leaf memories with this leaf-rubbing project.

YOU WILL NEED

- Plain paper

- A hard flat surface, such as a clipboard, a thick piece of cardboard, or a flat book

- Crayons with the paper removed

- Masking tape (optional)

- Your feet and hands!

WHAT TO DO

- Head outside with your supplies.

- Collect some interesting leaves. Fresh leaves work best! Dry, crispy leaves sometimes fall apart.

TIP
If your leaf is moving around under your paper, tape its stem to the flat surface.

- Place a leaf on your flat surface.

- Cover it with your plain piece of paper.

- Then, holding your crayon longways, rub it over the paper and the leaf beneath. A picture of your leaf should begin to show up.

THE WORLD OF BUGS

Enter the world of bugs.

Bugs are everywhere! Hopping, jumping, crawling, flying — these tiny members of our world are food for all kinds of creatures. They help dead animals and plants turn back into soil. They spread pollen from flower to flower. This helps plants to grow.

So many bugs live in our world! Here are some you might see outside:

BUTTERFLIES AND MOTHS

These flying insects have wings and six legs. Their long tongue helps them reach into flowers to gather sweet nectar. They carry pollen from flower to flower on their legs.

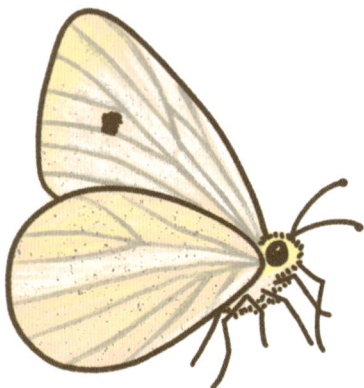

BEES

Bees are some of nature's most important pollinators. You might recognise them from their yellow-and-black bodies and clear wings. Bees tend to sting only if they feel threatened by people or other animals.

WASPS

Wasps come in all shapes and sizes. Some are yellow and black, others are brown, and still others are just black. Wasps have wings and six legs. Some have wings that are clear, and others have wings that are brown or black. Wasps are pollinators, like bees.

BEETLES

Beetles have a hard shell and six legs. Most of these insects can fly. Beetles can be big or tiny, plain or brightly coloured. Ladybirds are a common type of beetle.

CENTIPEDES

Centipedes have way more than six legs — they have anywhere from 15 to 77 pairs of legs! These fast runners have long, wiggly bodies. They are nocturnal, meaning they are active at night. Centipedes eat other small creatures, like insects, worms and spiders.

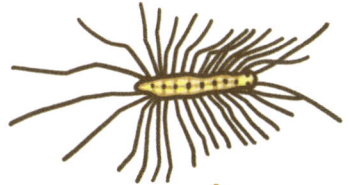

SPIDERS

Spiders are not insects. Instead, they belong to a group called arachnids. This bug has eight legs — and eight pairs of eyes! Many types of spiders spin some sort of web. Spiders catch and eat insects and other small animals.

ANTS

Busy ants can be black, brown or reddish. You can often see these strong insects carrying bits of dirt, wood, leaves or other dead insects. Ants have six legs and three body sections, like all insects. They live in big groups called colonies.

MY OBSERVATIONS...

(circle one)

bugs in a group   a bug alone

I saw my bug in or on: _____

_____

_____

The weather was: _____

_____

_____

The season was: _____

_____

_____

My bug was bigger than a small coin: yes   no

My bug was smaller than a small coin: yes   no

Here is a picture of my bug:

My bug's markings are: _____

_____

_____

When I saw my bug, it was: _____

_____

_____

MY OBSERVATIONS...

(circle one)

bugs in a group   a bug alone

I saw my bug in or on: _____

_____

_____

The weather was: _____

_____

_____

The season was: _____

_____

_____

My bug was bigger than a small coin: yes   no

My bug was smaller than a small coin: yes   no

Here is a picture of my bug:

My bug's markings are: _____

_____

_____

When I saw my bug, it was: _____

_____

_____

MY OBSERVATIONS...

(circle one)

bugs in a group   a bug alone

I saw my bug in or on: _____

_____

_____

The weather was: _____

_____

_____

The season was: _____

_____

_____

My bug was bigger than a small coin: yes   no

My bug was smaller than a small coin: yes   no

Here is a picture of my bug:

My bug's markings are: _____

_____

_____

When I saw my bug, it was: _____

_____

_____

MY OBSERVATIONS...

(circle one)

bugs in a group   a bug alone

I saw my bug in or on: _____

_____

_____

The weather was: _____

_____

_____

The season was: _____

_____

_____

My bug was bigger than a small coin: yes   no

My bug was smaller than a small coin: yes   no

Here is a picture of my bug:

My bug's markings are: _____

_____

_____

When I saw my bug, it was: _____

_____

_____

MY OBSERVATIONS...

(circle one)

bugs in a group   a bug alone

I saw my bug in or on: _____

_____

_____

The weather was: _____

_____

_____

The season was: _____

_____

_____

My bug was bigger than a small coin: yes   no

My bug was smaller than a small coin: yes   no

Here is a picture of my bug:

My bug's markings are: _____

_____

_____

When I saw my bug, it was: _____

_____

_____

BUG MAPPING

Make a bug map! Bugs are busy creatures. Be a bug detective and trace its movements.

YOU WILL NEED

- Plain paper

- A hard flat surface, such as a clipboard, a thick piece of cardboard, or a flat book

- Something to write with

WHAT TO DO

- Pick a comfy outdoor spot, such as a garden or a park. You will need to sit down, so make sure you're in a safe area.

- Now, draw a map of your spot, including trees, bushes, rocks – anything around you.

- Wait until you spot a bug.

- Now, watch the bug's path and draw it on your map. When you're done, you'll have a record of the bug's movements.

TIP
Crawling or walking insects are best for this activity! Flying insects tend to move too quickly.

NATURE CLOSE TO HOME

Hiking is exciting. Going on nature adventures is fun, too. But you can also be a nature explorer right at home. You can explore your garden, your balcony or deck, or even your windowsill!

Get your eyes ready to examine the sky and the ground. Get your ears ready to listen and your nose ready to smell. If you're exploring nature in a garden, you can lie down in the grass. What do you see down there with the roots and the insects?

Are you sitting on a deck or a balcony? Use your eyes and ears. Do you see birds? How about squirrels running up trees? And if you don't have a place where you can go outside, just open a window. Smell the air — is it flowery, snowy or smoky? How about the wind? Can you feel the breeze on your face? Nature is always close by, no matter where you live.

MY OBSERVATIONS...

Here's where I am right now:

back garden   front garden   porch   deck   patio

balcony   in front of a window

The time of day is: _____

_____

The season is: _____

_____

The weather right now is: _____

_____

Here is a list of all the nature things I can see: _____

_____

_____

I can also hear: _____

_____

_____

And I can smell: _____

_____

_____

Here is a picture of one plant, animal or rock that I can see right now:

MY OBSERVATIONS...

Here's where I am right now:

back garden   front garden   porch   deck   patio

balcony   in front of a window

The time of day is: _____

_____

The season is: _____

_____

The weather right now is: _____

_____

Here is a list of all the nature things I can see: _____

_____

_____

I can also hear: _____

_____

_____

And I can smell: _____

_____

_____

Here is a picture of one plant, animal or rock that I can see right now:

MY OBSERVATIONS...

Here's where I am right now:

back garden   front garden   porch   deck   patio

balcony   in front of a window

The time of day is: _____

_____

The season is: _____

_____

The weather right now is: _____

_____

Here is a list of all the nature things I can see: _____

_____

_____

I can also hear: _____

_____

_____

And I can smell: _____

_____

_____

Here is a picture of one plant, animal or rock that I can see right now:

MY OBSERVATIONS...

Here's where I am right now:

back garden   front garden   porch   deck   patio

balcony   in front of a window

The time of day is: _____

_____

The season is: _____

_____

The weather right now is: _____

_____

Here is a list of all the nature things I can see: _____

_____

_____

I can also hear: _____

_____

_____

And I can smell: _____

_____

_____

Here is a picture of one plant, animal or rock that I can see right now:

MY OBSERVATIONS...

Here's where I am right now:

back garden   front garden   porch   deck   patio

balcony   in front of a window

The time of day is: _____

_____

The season is: _____

_____

The weather right now is: _____

_____

Here is a list of all the nature things I can see: _____

_____

_____

I can also hear: _____

_____

_____

And I can smell: _____

_____

_____

Here is a picture of one plant, animal or rock that I can see right now:

MAKE A MUD FACE!

Get silly — and a little messy — and create a nature sculpture.

YOU WILL NEED

- A good clump of soft mud or clay
- Twigs, grass, blossoms, pebbles, pieces of moss – any 'bits' from nature

GET SCULPTING!

- Form your mud or clay blob into a flattish circle.

- Then, make a face on your blob using your nature bits. Don't forget hair and eyebrows!

TIP
A tree trunk works well for displaying your mud faces!

NATURE ON PAPER

Now that you've spent time in nature, try writing about it! Many poets and authors have felt inspired to write about nature. Check out the first verse of this poem by English poet William Wordsworth:

I wandered lonely as a Cloud
That floats on high o'er Vales and Hills,
When all at once I saw a crowd,
A host of golden Daffodils;
Beside the Lake, beneath the trees,
Fluttering and dancing in the breeze.

The American poet Emily Dickinson also liked to write about what she saw in nature. Here, she writes about watching a bird:

A Bird, came down the Walk —
He did not know I saw —
He bit an Angle Worm in halves
And ate the fellow, raw . . .

What do you enjoy seeing in nature? Have you seen a funny-shaped rock? Or a beautiful sunset? Have you been outside when a storm is coming? Writing poems and stories about nature can be a great way to capture these memories.

Pick an object or moment from your nature exploration. Remember that poems and stories aren't just about pretty things! Did you see something scary? Or sad? Or gross? It's okay to write about these things. And don't forget the illustration, too!

MY OBSERVATIONS...

My nature poem/story will be about: _____

_____

_____

_____

Here are three words that describe my object or moment:

_____

_____

_____

This object or moment makes me feel: _____

_____

_____

_____

Here is my nature poem/story:

MY OBSERVATIONS...

My nature poem/story will be about: _____

_____

_____

_____

Here are three words that describe my object or moment:

_____

_____

_____

This object or moment makes me feel: _____

_____

_____

_____

Here is my nature poem/story:

MY OBSERVATIONS...

My nature poem/story will be about: _____

_____

_____

_____

Here are three words that describe my object or moment:

_____

_____

_____

This object or moment makes me feel: _____

_____

_____

_____

Here is my nature poem/story:

MY OBSERVATIONS...

My nature poem/story will be about: _____

_____

_____

_____

Here are three words that describe my object or moment:

_____

_____

_____

This object or moment makes me feel: _____

_____

_____

_____

Here is my nature poem/story:

MY OBSERVATIONS...

My nature poem/story will be about: _____

_____

_____

_____

Here are three words that describe my object or moment:

_____

_____

_____

This object or moment makes me feel: _____

_____

_____

_____

Here is my nature poem/story:

MY OBSERVATIONS...

My nature poem/story will be about: _____

_____

_____

_____

Here are three words that describe my object or moment:

_____

_____

_____

This object or moment makes me feel: _____

_____

_____

_____

Here is my nature poem/story:

MAKE YOUR OWN BOOK

Now that you've written several poems or stories, make a book of your writing and decorate the cover.

YOU WILL NEED

- Plain paper

- Glue

- Markers, coloured pencils or crayons

- Twigs, grass, blossoms, dry moss – any 'bits' from nature

- A stapler and help from an adult

WHAT TO DO

- Copy your poems or stories from your journal onto the plain paper.

- On another plain sheet of paper, glue your nature bits into interesting patterns and shapes. This will be your cover.

- Wait for the glue to dry.

- Add a title and illustrations to your book.

- With help from an adult, staple your pages together along the long side to make a book.

KEEP EXPLORING!

Use these blank pages to do more writing or drawing.

MAP IT OUT:

RECORD YOUR EXPLORING ROUTES

Draw your nature maps here, so you can go exploring in those spots again — or just so you can create nature memories.

Author: Emma Carlson Berne
Project Editor: Priyanka Lamichhane
Designer & Illustrator: Kelly Abeln
Publishing Director: Piers Pickard
Publisher: Rebecca Hunt
Art Director: Emily Dubin
Print Production: Nigel Longuet

Published in May 2025 by Lonely Planet Global Limited
CRN: 554153
ISBN: 9781837584772
www.lonelyplanet.com/kids
© Lonely Planet 2025
10 9 8 7 6 5 4 3 2 1
Printed in China

All rights reserved. No part of this publication may be reproduced, stored in a retrieval system
or transmitted in any form by any means, electronic, mechanical, photocopying, recording or
otherwise except brief extracts for the purpose of review, without the written permission of the
publisher. Lonely Planet and the Lonely Planet logo are trademarks of Lonely Planet and are
registered in the US Patent and Trademark Office and in other countries.

Although the author and Lonely Planet have taken all reasonable care in preparing this book,
we make no warranty about the accuracy or completeness of its content and, to the maximum
extent permitted, disclaim all liability from its use.
STAY IN TOUCH
lonelyplanet.com/contact

Lonely Planet Office:
IRELAND
Digital Depot, Roe Lane (off Thomas St), Digital Hub, Dublin 8, D08 TCV4, Ireland

FSC
www.fsc.org

MIX
Paper | Supporting
responsible forestry
FSC™ C021741

Paper in this book is certified against the
Forest Stewardship Council™ standards.
FSC™ promotes environmentally responsible,
socially beneficial and economically viable
management of the world's forests.